ISBN 978-1-5281-4110-9
PIBN 10922235

1 MONTH OF
FREE
READING

at

www.ForgottenBooks.com

By purchasing this book you are eligible for one month membership to ForgottenBooks.com, giving you unlimited access to our entire collection of over 1,000,000 titles via our web site and mobile apps.

To claim your free month visit:

www.forgottenbooks.com/free922235

Historic, archived document

Do not assume content reflects current
scientific knowledge, policies, or practices.

E. L. DEMMON

HOW CAN RESEARCH HELP THE MICHIGAN TIMBERLAND OWNER?[2]

E. L. Demmon, Director

Introduction

For several decades, Michigan produced more lumber than any other state. Its magnificent forests did much to build up the state as a great economic entity and were the source of much of the raw material for construction throughout the Midwest.

Now the virgin forests are about gone, but Michigan still has the land, the climate, and the second-growth forests to support existing dependent forest industries if the forests are skillfully managed for wood production. They can gradually supplant much of the costly long-haul, shipped-in wood supply if an effective program of applied forest land management is pursued by all owners, public and private.

Michigan is one of the most highly industrialized areas in the United States. It uses enormous quantities of wood in its 1,600 and more primary and secondary wood-using plants. These plants employ about 60,000 workers, with pay rolls of over $80,000,000 annually. Wood products harvested each year in Michigan are worth approximately $10,000,000 on the stump. The annual value of the products processed from wood is over $400,000,000. These products come from sawmills, veneer and plywood mills, cooperage plants, planing mills, pulp, paper, and paperboard mills, and establishments using the products of these plants for a multitude of manufactured items.

There is a great deficit in wood production within the state, however, and large amounts must be shipped in from long distances. Actually, two-thirds of the forest raw materials now used are imported. Better forest practice is urgently needed to balance Michigan's forest budget.

Forest Area

At present, nineteen of Michigan's 37 million acres are forest land. When parks and noncommercial forest are eliminated, there remain over 17 million acres of commercial forest land. The class of forest growth occupying this land at present is shown in table 1.

1/ Maintained at University Farm, St. Paul, Minnesota, in cooperation with the University of Minnesota.

2/ Address before the Forestry Section, 51st Annual Meeting of the Michigan Academy of Science, Arts, and Letters, at Ann Arbor, Michigan, March 21, 1947.

Table 1.- Forest area by class of timber growth, 1945

Class of forest growth	:	Upper Peninsula	:	Lower Peninsula	:	State total	
		M acres	Percent	M acres	Percent	M acres	Percent
Saw timber		2,040	23	730	9	2,770	16
Pole timber		1,760	20	1,975	23	3,735	21
Restocking		3,600	41	3,475	40	7,075	41
Poorly stocked or denuded		1,420	16	2,380	28	3,300	22
TOTAL		8,820	100	8,560	100	17,380	100

Forest Landownership

In spite of widespread tax default in the past, almost two-thirds of Michigan's commercial forest land remain in private ownership. Furthermore, private owner-ship accounts for over 95 percent of the remaining saw-timber volume. Ownership of land and saw-timber stumpage are shown in table 2:

Table 2.- Ownership of commercial forest land and saw timber, 1945

Type of owner	:	Forest land	:	Saw-timber volume	
		Thousands of acres	Percent	Million bd.ft.	Percent
Private					
Industry and other		7,850	45.2	21,550	89.3
Farmers		3,260	18.8	1,500	6.2
Total private		11,110	64.0	23,050	95.5
State		4,050	23.3	650	2.7
County and municipal		65	.3	10	---
Federal					
National forest		2,035	11.7	405	1.7
Indian		20	.1	10	---
Other		100	.6	15	.1
Total federal		2,155	12.4	430	1.8
All owners		17,380	100.0	24,140	100.0

Volume of Saw Timber and Pulpwood

Although Michigan is usually thought of as a great pine state, by far the greater part of its remaining saw-timber stands is hardwood. Volumes of the principal species of saw timber and pulpwood are given in tables 3 and 4.

Table 3.- <u>Volume</u>[1]/ of principal saw-timber species, 1945

Species	Upper Peninsula		Lower Peninsula		State total	
	Million bd.ft.	Percent	Million bd.ft.	Percent	Million bd.ft.	Percent
Hemlock	4,408		152		4,560	
Spruce-fir	1,460		50		1,510	
White & red pine	772		318		1,090	
Jack pine	45		85		130	
Other softwoods	65		45		110	
Total softwoods	6,750	35	650	13	7,400	31
Sugar maple	5,280		430		5,710	
Yellow birch	2,565		35		2,600	
Aspen	1,037		853		1,890	
Elm	450		880		1,330	
Beech	830		340		1,170	
Basswood	780		280		1,060	
Oak	50		830		880	
Other hardwoods	1,348		752		2,100	
Total hardwoods	12,340	65	4,400	87	16,740	69
All species	19,090	100	5,050	100	24,140	100

1/ Volume of trees over 9 inches d.b.h. contained in logs at least 10 feet long; 6-inch minimum top diameter for aspen and softwoods, 8 inches for hardwoods.

Table 4.- <u>Volume of principal pulpwood species, 1945</u>

Pulpwood species	Standard pulpwood[1]/				In sawlog: Sub-size[2]/ material	Sub-standard pulpwood[3]/
	Upper Peninsula	Lower Peninsula	State total	Per-cent		
	M cords	M cords	M cords		M cords	M cords
Spruce	2,038	278	2,316	14	2,300	200
Balsam fir	3,694	370	4,064	25	1,300	900
Jack pine	288	800	1,088	7	300	200
Hemlock	2,399	124	2,523	15	9,600	3,600
Aspen	2,308	4,156	6,464	39	4,500	9,700
Total	10,727	5,728	16,455	100	18,000	14,600

1/ Material in trees 5 inches to 9 inches d.b.h. with at least two 100-inch pulpwood sticks and tops of sawlog trees, to a minimum diameter of 4 inches.
2/ Approximate cordwood equivalent (2¼ cords per M bd.ft.) of merchantable sawlogs 6 inches and larger in diameter, in trees over 9 inches in diameter.
3/ Cull sawlogs, substandard pulpwood sticks, and volume of one-stick trees.

Growth and Drain

During World War II, Michigan forests were severely overcut. With a continuing demand for wood, further heavy drain on the forests can be anticipated. The relationship between recent drain and annual growth presents a rather unpromising picture for the future. Unless current cutting decreases, annual growth must continue to decline as it did between 1935 and 1945. Current growth and drain data are given in tables 5 and 6:

Table 5.- Current annual growth in commercial forests, 1935 and 1945

Year	All timber[1] growth	Saw timber[2] Total	Softwood	Hardwood	Pole timber[3] Total	Softwood	Hardwood
	Million cu.ft.	Million bd.ft.			M cords		
1935	323	580	163	418	2,220	270	1,950
1945	295	519	96	423	2,061	291	1,770
		Percent decrease in 10 years					
	9	11			7		

1/ All trees 5 inches and over in diameter.
2/ All trees 9 inches and over in diameter.
3/ All trees 5 inches to 9 inches in diameter.

Table 6.- Drain by cutting and other causes, 1944

Item	Per-cent	All timber drain	Saw-timber drain Total	Soft-wood	Hard-wood	Pole-timber drain Total	Soft-wood	Hard-wood
		Million cu.ft.	Million bd.ft.			Thousands of cords		
Lumber	52	157.6	571.0	173.2	397.8	45.3	20.0	25.5
Pulpwood	20	59.1	130.0	114.2	15.8	320.0	277.3	42.7
Fuelwood	8	23.8	27.8	.7	27.1	217.3	---	217.3
Veneer	5	13.7	50.7	1	50.6	13.6	---	13.6
Mine timbers	3	10.4	27.8	12 7	15.1	38.7	34.7	4.0
Posts	2	6.0	5.4	:1	5.3	61.0	26.3	34.7
Other	5	15.6	49.2	3.0	46.2	31.7	13.2	18.5
Subtotal	95	286.2	861 9	304.0	557.9	727.6	371.5	356.1
Fire	(1/)	.4	1:2	.3	.9	.8	.5	.3
Other losses2/	5	15.1	39.1	12.7	26.4	61.0	21.8	39.2
Subtotal	5	15.5	40.3	13.0	27.3	61.8	22.3	39.5
Total drain	100	301.7	902.2	317.0	585.2	789.4	393.8	395.6
Avg.annual drain for 1935-44 incl.		283.9	801.0					

1/ Less than one-half of 1 percent.
2/ Losses from insects, disease, wind, etc.

-4-

Character of Timber Cutting

Sound land-use management is essential if forests are to yield the timber, wildlife, and recreational values inherent in them. Under good management, yields
from Michigan forests could at least be doubled. In some cases the game crop
will be of greater value than the trees. That most Michigan forests are not yet
being operated under good timber-harvesting practices is revealed in a study made
by the U. S. Forest Service in 1945. For all types of commercial forest landownership, only 35 percent of recent cutting could be rated as good or better,
17 percent fair, 44 percent poor, and 4 percent destructive. Less than 10 percent
of the current cutting on private land was rated good or better, whereas a high
proportion of cutting on national and state forests was rated at least good.

Federal Forest Research

Forest research provides the scientific basis for growing continuous crops of
timber and promoting the full use of forest land. The need and importance of
forest research as a public service were not fully recognized by the Federal
Government until May 1928, with the passage of the McSweeney-McNary Forest
Research Act. As far back as 1908, however, a limited amount of forest research
had been started by the U. S. Forest Service, and in July 1923, a forest experiment station was set up for the Lake States region, with an initial annual appro-
priation of $23,555. Headquarters were established at the University of Minnesota,
to serve the three states of Minnesota, Wisconsin, and Michigan. This station is
one of eleven regional stations maintained in the continental United States, in
addition to the Forest Products Laboratory at Madison, Wisconsin, which serves
the entire country.

Each forest experiment station works on the problems of an entire region and
covers silvicultural or forest management investigations; the effect of forests
on erosion, streamflow and floods; forest economics studies, including the
Forest Survey; and to a minor extent investigations of forest products. The
stations are responsible directly to the Assistant Chief of the Forest Service
in charge of research at Washington, D. C., and are separate from the adminis-
trative organization of the Forest Service, although the work of these two
field branches is closely coordinated. Research in forest biology is conducted
by biologists of the United States Fish and Wildlife Service who are headquartered
at the Lake States Station. Forest pathologists and forest entomologists have
been assigned to some of the regional forest experiment stations to work on
forest disease and insect problems.

In general, forest research is a job for public agencies because, first, it is
inefficient as well as expensive for each forest landowner to undertake research
for his individual land; secondly, the public is by far the largest single owner
of forest land; and finally, a long-time undertaking such as forest research
needs stability of program which public agencies can best provide. To help
rebuild Michigan's forests, there is need for an increased coordinated forest
research program, with federal and state forestry agencies, forestry schools,
forest industries, and other interested organizations cooperating closely for
that purpose. Michigan is fortunate in having developed in the past a strong
cooperative approach to its forest conservation problems, and the participation
of all the existing agencies through a Forest Research Advisory Council in
planning the general program and specific research projects from year to year
will insure a broad correlated attack and avoid unnecessary duplication.

The Federal Government portion of the program should be carried on from two research centers, one in the Upper Peninsula already functioning on a limited scale, and from a new center which is proposed for the Lower Peninsula. To date, 53 of these research centers have been established by the government throughout the forest areas of the United States. They are headquartered at locations convenient to the work and to the public.

The Forest Research Program Needed

Restocking the Land

Prior to the recent war, a total of close to 600,000 acres had been successfully planted to forest trees in Michigan by all agencies. Michigan led every state in the Union in this respect. Yet this is only about one-sixth of what remains to be done, according to recent estimates shown in table 7:

Table 7.- Estimated future planting needs, 1947

Type of planting needed	Upper Peninsula	Lower Peninsula	State total
	M acres		
On denuded land	476	1,152	1,628
Converting "offsite" aspen	356	815	1,171
Partial planting in understocked areas	503	594	1,097
Total	1,335	2,561	3,896
Percent of forest area	(15)	(30)	(22)

Additional study is needed to show the best ways to restock this land for timber production, wildlife, and recreational purposes. This involves further studies of such matters as methods of ground preparation, mechanized planting, spacings for different tree species and products, kinds and degrees of tree mixtures, methods and timing of aftercare, nursery techniques for hardwoods and game food species particularly, and the practicability of planting trees for fire breaks.

Management of Pine

There are over 1½ million acres of pine forest type (about 70 percent of it jack pine) in Michigan. Much of this is producing only a fraction of the wood of which it is capable. Research is needed to determine how best to insure adequate natural reproduction, how and when to make harvest cuts, and how to make intermediate cuts, which should go far in supplying local pulp and paper mills with much needed raw material, a major part of which is now being imported into the state from Canada and Minnesota. Studies will aim to show the best timing, methods, and intensities of thinning to foster various products, the best combination of mechanical and silvicultural measures to induce natural reproduction, and similar problems.

Northern Hardwood Problems

There are about 5 million acres of northern hardwoods in Michigan: maple, beech, basswood, birch, etc. Yet going industries ship in many of their supplies of these woods from other states. Much additional research is needed to point out the best ways of restoring high-quality northern hardwood forests and managing them to provide a continuous supply for industrial plants, chief among which is the furniture industry. This includes tests to find the proper time and method of making improvement cuttings to favor the more valuable species, how heavy and how often thinnings should be made and how to improve density of understocked stands.

Aspen Studies

Aspen covers nearly 6 million acres of Michigan. Notwithstanding new uses and an increased demand for aspen wood, only a small part of this vast area is producing wood of commercial value. How may the quality of aspen be improved, how early, how often, and how heavy should thinnings be made, what are the best means of converting low-quality aspen to better types? Will it pay? These are questions which need study.

Spruce, Fir, Tamarack, and Cedar

Exceedingly complex problems are found in the management of these extensive and important pulpwood and pole types. Spruce-fir forests occupy nearly 1½ million acres in Michigan. Swamp forests of spruce, tamarack, and cedar occupy an additional 1½ million acres.

Bottomland Hardwood Types

One million acres of stream bottom and other lowland forests of elm, ash, willow, cottonwood, and associated species can be made to contribute much, to farm land-owners in particular, if the most efficient forms of management can be worked out and put into practice.

Use of Oak Lands

Nearly one million acres of lower Michigan are covered with oak, much of it scrubby, its major use now being for fuelwood. Studies should be made to learn how existing stands can be improved. Hand in hand with a management project should go a study to develop new uses of oak and to find markets for the new products. Studies are needed to determine how far protection, improvement cutting, planting, etc., can improve understocked stands, how best to regenerate oak, and how and under what conditions oak stands should be converted to other species.

Economic and Marketing Studies

Other investigations which can be effectively tied in with a forest research program in Michigan include:

1. Study of the costs of timber growing and harvesting to provide a basis for intelligent planning of both public and private forest undertakings.

2. Market surveys pointed specifically at developing wider outlets for aspen, oak, and lower grades of other species. In particular, what use can be made of these species in the furniture and other local wood-using industries?

3. Logging and hauling experiments, with time and cost studies applied to various types of equipment, under varying conditions.

Farm Forestry

Many Michigan farms depend upon forest products for a portion of their income. The educational service available on farm forest problems has been greatly strengthened and extended in recent years. Farmers also could benefit greatly by additional research and demonstration areas where they could see and learn at first hand better methods of handling their woods. This would include examples of thinnings, improvement cuttings, harvest cuttings, protection from livestock, and artificial and natural regeneration methods.

Forest Fire Studies

In recent years, forest fire losses in Michigan have been relatively small. This has been due mainly to improved fire control, but a cycle of relatively wet years and a lessening of fire danger resulting from fewer slashings and land-clearing operations have also been a contributing factor. On the 18 million acres of state and private forest land under cooperative fire protection, the fire record for recent years is shown in table 8.

Table 8.- Forest fire record on State and private forest land in Michigan, 1939 to 1946 inclusive.

Year	Number of fires	Area burned	Cost per acre protected
		Acres	Cents
1939	1,172	47,071	.035
1940	899	17,388	.037
1941	1,604	10,462	.041
1942	807	14,905	.040
1943	723	18,563	.042
1944	1,484	22,254	.059
1945	959	22,881	.057
1946	1,923	23,138	.065

Although this fire control record is excellent, greater losses can be expected in years of serious fire hazard. Research has contributed to improving the effectiveness of fire control by (1) supplying basic information on fire occurrence, behavior, damage, and methods of control, (2) classifying fuels as to rate of spread and resistance to control, and (3) developing methods of measuring and anticipating fire danger. Additional research can assist in improving techniques and in analyzing past records as a basis for better appraisal of fire hazard, inflammability, and risk.

Forest Utilization Service

Within the last three years, forest utilization service units have been established in every major forest region of the United States except the Lake States. These units serve as a liaison service between the Forest Products Laboratory at Madison, Wisconsin, and the wood-using industries of the respective regions. Their function is to study the forest resources from the standpoint of industrial use, determine what can be done to improve forest utilization practices locally in the light of most recent technological developments, and transmit problems to the Forest Products Laboratory which can best be solved there. This type of service could be provided Michigan and the other two Lake states at a cost of about $30,000 annually. The men assigned to it would work out of the Lake States Forest Experiment Station, and would cooperate with the individual states and forest industries, to secure better forest utilization. Among important utilization problems needing solution are those dealing with the use of aspen and scrub hardwoods which dominate about 40 percent of the present forest area.

Forest Research Centers for Michigan

The purpose of forest research centers is to carry out research in forest management in its broadest sense as applied to local conditions. It includes studies of silviculture, reforestation, timber harvest and regeneration, and the economics of timber growing and marketing. To carry on forest research most effectively and to make it of maximum value to local industries and timberland owners, a separate research unit is needed for each section of the country having distinct forestry problems.

Research centers are needed in both the Upper and Lower Peninsula because climate, timber types, and economic conditions are so different in these two areas. Most of the investigations needed should be made on experimental forests located on publicly owned lands, representative of the major forest types and conditions found in the state. With over 6 million acres in state and national forests in Michigan, opportunities as well as need to establish studies on public lands are unequaled.

An effective federal forest research center to carry out such a cooperative forest research program can be developed with an annual budget of about $50,000. This would cover fixed charges, field operating expenses, salaries of technicians, student field assistants, and wages for laborers. It should be administered by the Lake States Forest Experiment Station, supplemented by cooperative funds and personnel from state and other agencies.

Michigan forests have suffered from heavy wartime demands. They must be rebuilt if they are to meet the needs of increasing industrial development. Forest research can show the way to substantial rural and industrial prosperity through improved use of all forest land. Every Michigan citizen will profit from a well-rounded program of forest research.

CPSIA information can be obtained
at www.ICGtesting.com
Printed in the USA
BVHW071429231118
533754BV00031B/3894/P

9 781528 141109